Lewis & Clark

Lewis & Clark

by Francene Sabin
Illustrated by John Lawn

Troll

Library of Congress Cataloging-in-Publication Data

Sabin, Francene.
   Lewis and Clark.

   Summary: Discusses the contribution made by the two
men who in 1804–05 led an exploring expedition across
the Oregon Territory to the Pacific Ocean.
   1. Lewis and Clark Expedition—Juvenile literature.
2. Lewis, Meriwether, 1774–1809—Juvenile literature.
3. Clark, William, 1770–1838—Juvenile literature.
4. United States—Exploring expeditions—Juvenile
literature.   5. West (U.S.)—Description and travel—
To 1848—Juvenile literature.   [1. Lewis, Meriwether,
1774–1809.   2. Clark, William, 1770–1838.   3. Lewis
and Clark Expedition.   4. Explorers.   5. United States—
Exploring expeditions.   6. West (U.S.)—Discovery and
exploration]   I. Lawn, John, ill.   II. Title.
F592.7.S115   1984   917.8'042   84-2642
ISBN 0-8167-0224-1 (lib. bdg.)
ISBN 0-8167-0225-X (pbk.)

This edition published in 2002.

Printed in the United States of America.

10 9 8 7 6 5 4 3 2

At the start of the nineteenth century, the United States was still a small nation. But a number of Americans were beginning to look west, across the great expanse of uncharted wilderness. Among them were two daring and resourceful soldiers, Meriwether Lewis and William Clark. These men did more than dream about that wilderness. In 1804, they led an expedition that opened the door to the vast country between the Mississippi River and the Pacific Ocean.

For three years, Lewis and Clark and the small group they led traveled through the western lands, exploring the Great Plains and the Rocky Mountains. They met and made friends with many tribes of American Indians. They collected information about the animal life, the plant life, and the geography of this immense territory.

Meriwether Lewis was born near Charlottesville, Virginia, on August 18, 1774. Lewis had little formal education but he was an excellent hunter, fisherman, and outdoorsman. He enlisted in the Virginia militia at the age of twenty and soon after transferred to the regular army.

Lewis's leadership and military skills earned him the rank of captain and brought him to the attention of Thomas Jefferson. In 1801, when Jefferson became President of the United States, he offered Lewis a job as his private secretary. Lewis welcomed the opportunity to work closely with the brilliant statesman and patriot.

In the following two years, Jefferson and Lewis often talked about an overland expedition to the Pacific. It was Jefferson's dream to learn about the whole continent and to make it part of the United States. Meriwether Lewis was, in Jefferson's opinion, the perfect person to blaze the trail west. Congress agreed, and Lewis was given the assignment.

At the beginning of 1803, Meriwether Lewis began ordering the supplies necessary for the expedition. Once this was done, he went to Pennsylvania to study botany, zoology, and how to travel at night using only the stars to guide him.

In Philadelphia, he also bought scientific instruments, maps, and medical supplies. In addition, Lewis stocked up on beads, mirrors, and other items to use as gifts for the Native Americans.

Lewis's assignment was to learn all about the western American Indians and the possibility of trading with them. He was also to learn everything he could about minerals, soil, climate, weather, wildlife, and anything else that might be of use in the future. Lewis felt that it was an overwhelming task for one expedition leader and that he should share this leadership. His choice of co-leader was William Clark.

William Clark, the younger brother of George Rogers Clark, a hero of the American Revolution, was born in Caroline County, Virginia, on August 1, 1770. Like Lewis, he grew up as an active outdoorsman. Also like Lewis, Clark had served in the army of the young United States. And when his friend, Meriwether Lewis, offered him the co-leadership of a historic expedition, William Clark agreed at once.

In 1803, when the expedition was being formed, the United States consisted of seventeen states. All of them were in the eastern part of North America. At the same time, Americans were settling the open area east of the Mississippi River. The United States also had just purchased the Louisiana Territory from France. This territory extended from the Mississippi River to the Rocky Mountains and from Canada down to the Gulf of Mexico.

The Louisiana Purchase instantly doubled the size of American land holdings. But there was still a huge stretch of country between the Rockies and the Pacific Ocean. This land, called the Oregon Territory, would also belong to America one day. One of the purposes of the Lewis and Clark expedition was to strengthen America's claim to this land.

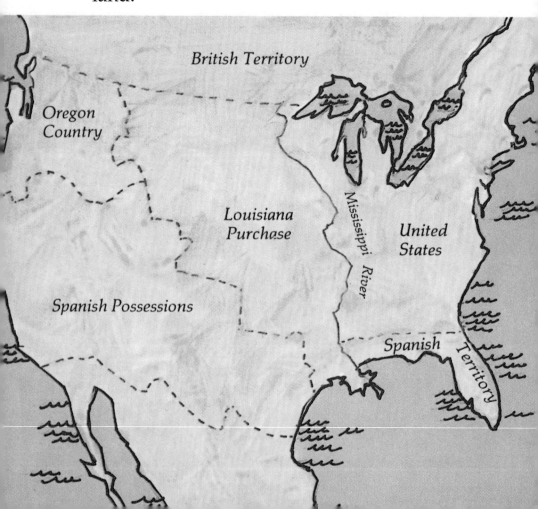

British Territory

Oregon
Country

Louisiana
Purchase

Mississippi River

United
States

Spanish Possessions

Spanish

Territory

Meriwether Lewis and William Clark assembled about forty rugged frontiersmen for the expedition. The group established a camp, in the winter of 1803, near St. Louis on the banks of the Mississippi River.

They built river boats and went through a tough training program. Lewis and Clark knew that the party would need to be highly disciplined and in top physical shape for the trip ahead.

On May 14, 1804, the expedition headed up the Missouri River. As the two leaders and several of the others noted in their journals, the trip was extremely difficult right from the start. They encountered swift river currents, shifting sandbars, heavy mud, hordes of mosquitoes, terrible storms, and blistering heat.

The expedition was constantly plagued by injuries and illnesses. It took the group over five difficult months to reach the place where the city of Bismarck, North Dakota, now stands.

The party built a log blockhouse, which they named Fort Mandan, because a tribe of Mandan Indians had a village nearby. The members of the expedition spent the winter there, making Fort Mandan the westernmost military post of the United States.

The winter of 1804 was spent hunting, making friends with the nearby Native Americans, and gathering information about the countryside. The co-leaders also made a very fortunate acquaintance with Toussaint Charbonneau, a French-Canadian scout, and his American Indian wife, Sacajawea. She was a Shoshone woman who had been kidnapped from her tribe when she was a young girl. Sacajawea and Charbonneau agreed to act as guides and interpreters for the expedition.

In April 1805, Lewis and Clark sent sixteen of their party back to St. Louis. This group was to convey to Thomas Jefferson the information and scientific specimens collected by the expedition. The remainder of the group resumed the journey west. By the beginning of May, they reached the southwestern corner of what is today the state of Montana.

It was in this area that they encountered their first grizzly bears. The Native Americans had warned them about the massiveness and ferocity of these beasts, but the group didn't take the warning seriously. Meeting the bears changed their minds. Some of the creatures stood eight-and-a-half feet tall, weighed more than five-hundred pounds, and had claws like huge daggers.

As Clark's journal recounts, one grizzly almost wiped out six hunters. Four of them hit the bear with rifle bullets, but the animal just whirled and charged them. The two other hunters fired, but the bear didn't even slow down. The six hunters fled, two of them jumping off a twenty-foot cliff into a river. The bear came right after them and didn't stop until a well-aimed bullet struck it in a vital spot.

Hunting buffalo was a great deal easier, safer, and more successful. It also supplied the travelers with a large portion of their food.

In midsummer of 1805, the expedition reached the eastern foothills of the Rocky Mountains. It was now that Sacajawea played an important part in keeping the expedition going. This was Shoshone territory, where she had lived as a child. The American Indians were wary of strangers. They might have attacked the expedition if Sacajawea had not been with it.

When the party met the Shoshone Indians, Sacajawea acted as interpreter and peacemaker. Through her efforts, the party was able to obtain horses to take them over the mountains. As Lewis and Clark soon learned, it wasn't possible to ride the horses over the rough and rugged Rockies. But the animals were extremely useful for carrying supplies, while the party went on foot.

Lewis and Clark had no idea of what to expect once they descended the western slopes of the Rockies. The maps of the time, based on guesswork rather than firsthand knowledge, were faulty. They showed that the expedition could expect a short, simple trip to the Pacific Ocean. However, this was far from the truth. There were many challenging miles still ahead of them.

It was November 1805, before the party sighted the blue-green waters of the Pacific. The weather was cold and wet. Rain fell day after day, but there was no time to rest.

Before winter set in, the party selected a campsite and built a log enclosure. They called it Fort Clatsop. The fort was named for the Clatsop Indians, who lived in that area and provided friendship and help to the expedition.

During the winter of 1805, Lewis and Clark mapped the surrounding land and worked on their scientific notes. In their notes, they described the Native Americans,

the animals, the plants, the soil, and the geography of the land. They wrote down everything they had seen since leaving Fort Mandan the previous spring.

At the end of March 1806, the expedition began its homeward journey. Six months later, on September 23, the group reached St. Louis. Their return was cause for great excitement. To the people in the East, Lewis and Clark's journey was as daring and inspiring as the first journey to the moon would be more than 150 years later.

Lewis and Clark returned from their expedition with an incomparable treasure. It wasn't gold or silver or diamonds. It was information—maps of rivers and mountains, forests and plains. It was drawings of animals, birds, reptiles, plants—almost all of them new to the eyes of Americans. And most important of all, their trip had made the development of the West a real possibility.

In the next few years, many trappers and mountain men followed in the footsteps of Lewis and Clark. They, in turn, were followed by the pioneers who traveled west on the Oregon Trail. And these wagon trains were followed by the railroad. In time, the United States stretched from the Atlantic to the Pacific. Meriwether Lewis and William Clark had helped make Thomas Jefferson's great dream come true!

Meriwether Lewis   *William Clark*